NINJA FOODI
COOKBOOK SPEEDI

With Pictures

By: Cara James

Table of Contents

BREAKFAST

LUNCH

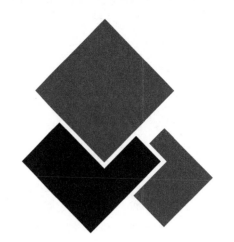

POULTRY

MEAT

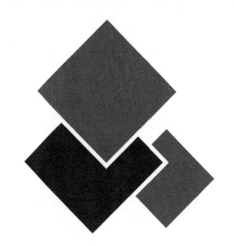

SEAFOOD

SIDE DISH

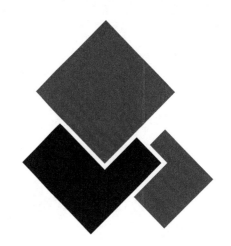

STARTERS

VEGETABLE

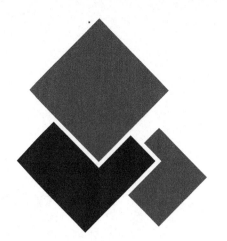

DESSERTS

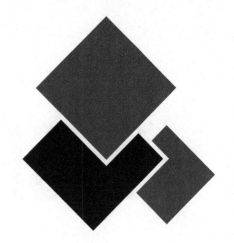

Breakfast
Recipes

Chapter: 1

Fantastic fried Potatoes

Preparation Steps:

1. Place the potatoes on the crisper tray in the bottom position and then add the paprika, pepper, salt, and oil and close the lid.
2. Flip the SmartSwitch to ARY FRY / STOVETOP, select BAKE / ROAST, set the temperature to 180°C, and set the time to Twenty minutes. Press START/STOP to start cooking and stir from time to time.
3. Finally, Transfer the potatoes to a bowl and add the coriander and yoghurt. Toss, serve and enjoy.

 Prep + Cooking Time: 25 mins

 Portions: 3

Ingredients:

- 680g cubed gold potatoes
- 113g Greek yogurt
- 30ml olive oil
- 6g sweet paprika
- 2g chopped coriander
- Salt & black pepper

Awesome scrambled Eggs

Preparation Steps:

1. Mix all ingredients in a bowl, and whisk well.
2. On the bottom of the unit, add a drizzle of olive oil and heat up, then pour the mixture and close the lid.
3. Flip the SmartSwitch™ to RAPID COOKER and select SEAR/SAUTE, set temperature to 115°C, stir and cook for ten mins. Serve right away

 Prep + Cooking Time: 15 mins

 Portions:3

Ingredients:

- Four whisked eggs
- A chopped red onion
- 4g sweet paprika
- A drizzle of olive oil
- Salt & black pepper

Runner Beans Omelet

Preparation Steps:

1. Mix all elements in a bowl, except the oil, and beans and whisk well.
2. Put the oil on the bottom of the unit and flip the SmartSwitch™ to RAPID COOKER, select SEAR/SAUTE, set the temperature to 160°C and Press START/STOP to heat it up.
3. Add the beans, stir and sauté them for three mins.
4. Next, add the egg mixture over the beans; spread and close the lid.
5. Set the time for seven to eight mins more. Slice the omelette and serve it immediately

Ingredients:

- 85g trimmed and halved Runner beans
- Four whisked eggs
- Four minced garlic cloves
- 3g soy sauce
- 15ml olive oil
- Salt & black pepper

 Prep + Cooking Time: 15 mins

 Portions: 5

Sausage Rolls

Preparation Steps:

1. Roll out the puff pastry on the work area, divide the cheese, sausage, and mustard, roll up tightly, and cut the crust into medium pieces.
2. Put the rolls on the crisper tray in the bottom position and close the lid. Flip the SmartSwitch™ to RAPID COOKER. Select STEAM, then set the temperature to 190°C set time for ten mins.
3. To begin cooking, press START/STOP. Plate the rolls after dividing them.

 Prep + Cooking Time: 20 mins

 Portions: 6

Ingredients:

- A sheet puff pastry
- Eightchopped sausage slices
- Four grated handful of gruyere cheese
- 20g mustard

Courgette and Chicken Tortillas

Preparation Steps:

1. In the beginning, spread the butter on the tortillas, put them on the crisper tray in the bottom position and close the lid.
2. Flip the SmartSwitch™ to RAPID COOKER and select STEAM set the temperature to 205°C and set the time to three mins.
3. Press START/STOP to begin cooking
4. Next, mix the mayo, mustard, chicken and courgette in a bowl and stir.
5. Finally, divide the mixture between the tortillas, sprinkle with cheese, roll them and continue cooking at 205°C for four mins more.
6. Serve and enjoy!

 Prep + Cooking Time: 12 mins

 Portions: 6

Ingredients:

- 170g cooked and shredded rotisserie chicken
- Four tortillas
- 75g mayonnaise
- 124g shredded courgette
- 100g grated parmesan cheese
- 55g softened butter
- 30g mustard

Hash Browns Breakfast

Preparation Steps:

1. On the bottom of the unit, add oil and heat it up at 175°C.
2. Next, add all other items and lock up the lid. Flip the SmartSwitch™ to AIR FRY/STOVETOP and select AIR FRY then set the time to twenty-five mins.
3. Finally, press START/STOP to begin cooking
4. Enjoy!

 Prep + Cooking Time: 30 mins

 Portions: 4

Ingredients:

- 680g hash browns
- Two eggs
- A chopped red pepper
- A chopped red onion
- 10ml vegetable oil
- 1g chopped thyme
- Salt & black pepper

Lunch
Recipes

Chapter: 2

cod Fillets and Kale Salad

Preparation Steps:

1. Season the fish with salt and pepper, then place it on the crisper tray in the bottom position.
2. Drizzle 10ml of oil over the fish and lock up the lid. Spin the SmartSwitch™ to ARY FRY/ STOVETOP. Select BAKE & ROAST, set the temperature to 205°C and set the time to ten mins.
3. Divide fish between plates.
4. Mix the remaining elements in a bowl and toss. Divide the salad next to the fish. Serve and enjoy!

 Prep + Cooking Time: 20 mins

 Portions: 4

Ingredients:

- Two boneless black cod fillets
- A thinly sliced fennel bulb
- 70g shredded kale leaves
- 65g pecans
- 151g halved grapes
- 30ml olive oil + 5ml.
- 10ml balsamic vinegar
- Salt & black pepper

Chicken Pizza Rolls

Preparation Steps:

1. Add the onion and half of the olive oil to the bottom of the unit.
2. Set the temperature to 205°C and flip the SmartSwitch™ to AIR FRY/ STOVETOP. Select AIR FRY, then fry and shake for eight mins.
3. Add the chicken, pepper, salt and Worcestershire sauce; toss. and continue frying for eight mins more, stirring once and then transfer to a bowl.
4. On your working surface, roll the pizza dough and shape it into a rectangle.
5. Spread the cheese all over, onion and chicken mixture, then the tomato sauce.
6. Roll the dough and place it on the crisper tray in the bottom position, brush the roll with the rest of the oil and close the lid.
7. Change the function to BAKE/ROAST.
8. Reset temperature to 190°C and time also to fourteen mins, then press START/STOP to continue cooking. Flipping the roll halfway
9. Slice your roll and serve.

Ingredients:

- Two skinless, boneless and sliced chicken breasts
- 400g pizza dough
- 45g grated parmesan cheese
- 110ml tomato sauce
- A sliced yellow onion
- 10ml olive oil
- 20ml Worcestershire sauce
- Salt & black pepper

 Prep + Cooking Time: 40 mins

 Portions: 9

Wonderful Hot Dogs

Preparation Steps:

1. Place the hot dogs on the crisper tray in the bottom position and lock up the lid.
2. Flip the SmartSwitch™ to AIR FRY/ STOVETOP. Select AIR FRY, set the temperature to 200°C, and set the time for five mins.
3. When the timer finishes, open the lid and put the hot dogs into the buns, spread the mustard all over and sprinkle with the parmesan.
4. Transfer the hot dogs to the crisper tray and reclose the lid and continue cooking at 200°C for three mins more. Enjoy!

Ingredients:

- Two hot dog buns
- Two hot dogs
- 10g grated parmesan cheese
- 15g Dijon mustard

 Prep + Cooking Time: 13 mins

 Portions: 4

Veggie Pudding

Preparation Steps:

1. Grease the butter in the bottom of the unit or use a Multi-Purpose Pan, and add all other items except the cheddar cheese and toss.
2. Sprinkle the cheese all over and close the lid, flip the SmartSwitch™ to AIR FRY/STOVETOP and select AIR FRY.
3. Set temperature to 180°C, then set time to thirty mins.
4. Serve and enjoy!!

 Prep + Cooking Time: 40 mins

 Portions: 4

Ingredients:

- 345g corn
- 120g Double cream
- 3 cups cubed bread
- 370ml milk
- 25g chopped celery
- 15ml softened butter
- Two chopped red peppers
- One chopped yellow onion
- 15g grated cheddar cheese
- 1g chopped thyme
- 5g minced garlic
- Three whisked eggs
- Salt & black pepper

Cod Meatballs

Preparation Steps:

1. Mix all ingredients except the oil in your food processor and blend well, then shape medium-sized meatballs out of this mixture.
2. Place the meatballs on the crisper tray in the bottom position, grease them with oil and close the lid.
3. Flip the SmartSwitch™ to AIR FRY/STOVETOP and select BAKE & ROAST.
4. Set the temperature to 160°C and also time to twelve mins, shaking halfway.
5. Serve and enjoy!!

Ingredients:

 Prep + Cooking Time: 20 mins

 Portions:3

- 455g skinless and chopped cod
- One chopped yellow onion
- An egg
- 20g minced fresh coriander
- 30g panko breadcrumbs
- Two minced garlic cloves
- 2g sweet paprika
- 0.5g ground oregano
- A drizzle of olive oil
- Salt & black pepper

Veggie Stew

Preparation Steps:

1. On the bottom of the unit, mix all components except the coriander, toss well and close the lid.
2. Flip the SmartSwitch™ to AIR FRY/STOVETOP and select SEAR/SAUTE set the temperature to 180°C, and set the time also to twenty mins.
3. Press START/STOP to start cooking. Finally, divide the stew between bowls and sprinkle the coriander on top as the last touch and serve.

 Prep + Cooking Time: 30 mins

 Portions: 3

Ingredients:

- 200g tomato paste
- Two roughly chopped tomatoes
- Two green peppers; cut into strips
- Two minced garlic cloves
- Two roughly chopped yellow onions
- Four halved lengthwise Courgettes
- A cubed Aubergine
- 1.5g dried oregano
- 5g sugar
- 1g dried basil
- 30ml olive oil
- 20g chopped Coriander
- Salt & black pepper

Poultry
Recipes

Chapter: 3

Salsa Verde Chicken Breast

Preparation Steps:

1. place all ingredients except the cheese on the bottom of the unit, and toss then lock up the lid.
2. Turn the SmartSwitchTM to AIR FRY/STOVETOP.
3. Choose BAKE & ROAST, set the temperature to 190°C, and cook this for 17 minutes.
4. To commence or stop cooking, press START/STOP. When the timer is completed, open the lid and sprinkle with the cheese and continue cooking for around three to four mins.
5. Divide between plates and serve.

Ingredients:

 Prep + Cooking Time: 30 mins

 Portions: 5

- 455g salsa Verde
- 455g boneless and skinless chicken breast
- 180g grated cheddar cheese
- 15g chopped parsley
- 2g sweet paprika
- 15ml avocado oil
- Salt & black pepper

Chicken Breasts and Veggies

Preparation Steps:

1. On the bottom of the unit, add a tablespoon of oil, onions, stir and cook for two mins, then add the peppers and mushrooms.
2. Rub the chicken breasts with the remaining of the oil and garlic then season with pepper and salt. Put the chicken breasts on the crisper tray in the elevated position and lock up the lid, flip the SmartSwitch™ to RAPID COOKER. Select SPEEDI MEALS, set temperature to 200°C and time to six mins. Press START/STOP to begin cooking. When the timer is completed, open the lid and put the mix aside, flip the breasts over the other side and continue cooking for six mins more.
3. Divide between plates, sprinkle the cheese all over and serve.

Ingredients:

- 910g chicken breasts; skinless and boneless
- Tweleve halved brown mushrooms
- A red onion
- A chopped red pepper
- One roughly chopped green pepper
- Two minced garlic cloves
- 30ml olive oil
- 30ml shredded cheddar cheese
- Salt & black pepper

 Prep + Cooking Time: 30 mins

 Portions: 5

Turkey and Parsley Pesto

Preparation Steps:

1. Blend the pepper, cranberry juice, garlic, salt, oil, maple syrup and parsley in your blender, pulse to make a parsley pesto and then transfer to a bowl.
2. Toss the turkey breasts into the bowl well and insert the bowl in the fridge for about a half-hour.
3. Drain the turkey breasts (retaining the parsley pesto), place them on the crisper tray in the bottom position and close the lid and flip the SmartSwitch™ to AIR FRY/STOVETOP. Select BAKE & ROAST, set the temperature to 195°C then set the time to thirty-five mins, flipping the meat halfway Finally, divide the turkey between plates, drizzle the parsley pesto, over the dish and serve.

 Prep + Cooking Time: 1H 5 mins

 Portions: 4

Ingredients:

- Two boneless, skinless and halved turkey breasts
- 60g chopped parsley
- 106ml olive oil
- 60ml Cranberry juice
- Four garlic cloves
- A drizzle of maple syrup
- A pinch of salt & black pepper

Chinese Style Chicken Thighs

Preparation Steps:

1. On the bottom of the pot, add sesame oil and olive over medium heat.
2. Add the onions, rice chillies, soy sauce, water, ginger, fish sauce and the Cranberry juice; whisk and cook for three to four mins
3. Next, add the chicken thighs and toss everything and close the lid.
4. Flip the SmartSwitch™ to AIR FRY/STOVETOP, select AIR FRY, set temperature to 200°C and set time to twenty-five mins.
   Divide between plates and serve.

 Prep + Cooking Time: 40 mins

 Portions: 4

Ingredients:

- Four chicken thighs
- A chopped bunch of spring onions
- 395ml water
- Two chopped green chillies
- 20g. fish sauce
- 15g soy sauce
- 15g cranberry juice
- 15ml olive oil
- 5g grated ginger
- 5ml sesame oil

Awesome Oregano Chicken Thighs

Preparation Steps:

1. Place all of the items in the bottom of the unit, mix well and lock up the lid.
2. Flip the SmartSwitch™ to AIR FRY/STOVETOP. Select BAKE & ROAST, set the temperature to 205°C, and set the time to thirty mins, shaking halfway.
   Divide between plates; serve

Prep + Cooking Time: 35 mins

Portions: 2

Ingredients:

- Eight chicken thighs
- Two minced garlic cloves
- A chopped red onion
- 4g chopped oregano
- 1g sweet paprika
- 30ml olive oil
- Salt & black pepper

Chicken and Green Coconut Sauce

Preparation Steps:

1. Blend the soy sauce with oil, five spice, green onion, pepper, garlic, salt, oyster sauce, ginger and coconut milk in your blender and pulse well.
2. On the bottom of the pot, combine the chicken with the green sauce, toss and close the lid.
3. Flip the SmartSwitch™ to AIR FRY/STOVETOP. Select BAKE & ROAST, set the temperature to 190°C, and set the time to sixteen mins; shaking once.
4. Sprinkle the parsley on top, drizzle the lemon juice also and serve.

 Prep + Cooking Time: 26 mins

 Portions: 4

Ingredients:

- Ten roughly chopped green onions
- Ten chicken drumsticks
- 250ml coconut milk
- 15g chopped parsley
- Four minced garlic cloves
- 30ml oyster sauce
- 45ml soy sauce
- 15ml lemon juice
- 5g grated ginger
- 3g Chinese five spice
- 5ml olive oil
- Salt & black pepper

Meat
Recipes

Chapter: 4

Beef and Peppers

Preparation Steps:

1. The Crisper Tray's legs should be pushed in, and it should be positioned at the bottom of the pot with all the ingredients underneath it before giving it a good toss.
2. Flip the SmartSwitch™ to AIR FRY/STOVETOP. Select BAKE & ROAST, set temperature to 200°C and set time to twenty-two mins. Press START/STOP to start cooking.
3. Divide the mix between plates and serve!

Ingredients:

  Prep + Cooking Time: 32 mins

Portions: 3

- 200g beef tenderloin; cut into strips
- A green pepper; cut into strips
- A yellow pepper; cut into strips
- A chopped sweet onion
- A red pepper; cut into strips
- 15ml olive oil
- Salt & black pepper

Lamb and Pepper

Preparation Steps:

1. In a pan that fits your Speedi Meal machine, place all the items and toss.
2. Place the pan in the machine and lock up the lid, flip the SmartSwitch™ to AIR FRY/STOVETOP. Select AIR FRY and set the temperature to 205°C, then set the time to twenty mins, press START/STOP to begin cooking; shaking the fryer halfway.
3. Divide everything between plates and serve

Ingredients:

 Prep + Cooking Time: 25 mins

 Portions: 3

- 455g lamb; cut into strips
- 120ml beef stock
- Four chopped shallots
- Two red peppers; cut into strips
- Four minced garlic cloves
- 15ml olive oil
- A pinch of salt & black pepper
- 30ml fish sauce

Beef and Mushroom

Preparation Steps:

1. On the bottom of the unit, place the crisper tray then combine and toss all ingredients well.
2. Lock up the lid and spin the SmartSwitch™ to AIR FRY/STOVETOP. Select AIR FRY, set the temperature to 200°C, and set the time to seventeen mins.
3. Divide everything between plates and serve

 Prep + Cooking Time: 22 mins

 Portions: 3

Ingredients:

- 225g sliced white mushrooms
- A chopped yellow onion
- Two beef steaks; cut into strips
- 35ml dark soy sauce
- 5ml olive oil
- Salt and black pepper to taste

Smoked lamb Roast

Preparation Steps:

1. In a bowl, mix all ingredients well and be sure the lamb is thoroughly coated.
2. Transfer the lamb to the crisper tray in the bottom position of the pot and lock up the lid.
3. Close the lid and flip the SmartSwitch™ to AIR FRY/STOVETOP, select BAKE & ROAST then set temperature to 190°C and time to fifty-five mins. Click START/STOP to begin cooking
4. Slice the roast, Enjoy!!

 Prep + Cooking Time: 1H

 Portions: 4

Ingredients:

- 910g lamb loin roast
- 5g chopped oregano
- 25g smoked paprika
- 15ml olive oil
- 5ml liquid smoke
- 15g Light brown sugar
- Salt & black pepper

Rubbed Steaks

Preparation Steps:

1. Rub the steaks with this mixture after combining all the spices in a bowl.
2. Put the steaks on the crisper tray in the bottom position, grease them with cooking spray and close the lid. Set the temperature to 190°C and time to seven mins on each side.
3. Click START/STOP to begin cooking.
4. Enjoy!

Ingredients:

  Prep + Cooking Time: 20 mins

Portions: 4

- 25g ancho chili powder
- Four flank steaks
- 5g grated ginger
- 5g dried oregano
- 5g dry mustard
- 5g sweet paprika
- 15g coriander; ground
  Cooking spray
- Salt & black pepper

Coconut beef

Preparation Steps:

1. On the bottom of the unit, mix all of the elements except the coconut milk; toss well and lock up the lid. Flip the SmartSwitch™ to RAPID COOKER. Select TEAM & CRISP, set temperature to 205°C and time to twelve mins; shaking halfway.
2. When the timer goes off, open the lid, pour in the coconut milk, stir, and simmer for an additional three to four minutes.
3. Serve everything after dividing it among bowls.

Ingredients:

 Prep + Cooking Time: 20 mins

 Portions: 3

- 200ml coconut milk
- 395g beef chops; cut into strips
- Two minced garlic cloves
- A chopped shallot
- 5g grated ginger
- 3g chili paste
- 30ml olive oil
- 45ml soy sauce
- Salt & black pepper

Seafood
Recipes

Chapter: 5

Shrimp and Veggies

Preparation Steps:

1. First, add all the items to a bowl and combine well.
2. Transfer everything to the bottom unit of the pot and lock up the lid.
3. Flip the SmartSwitch™ to AIR FRY/STOVETOP. Select AIR FRY, set the temperature to 160°C, and set the time for twenty mins, then click TART/STOP to begin cooking; shaking halfway. Divide between plates and serve

Ingredients:

  Prep + Cooking Time: 30 mins

Portions: 3

- 455g peeled and deveined shrimp
- 25g chopped red onion
- 155g chopped red pepper
- 105g chopped celery
- 15g. melted butter
- 2g sweet paprika
- 5ml Worcestershire sauce
- Salt & black pepper

Lemon salmon Fillets

Preparation Steps:

1. Merge the salmon with the other elements in a bowl, rub/coat well and transfer to the crisper tray in the bottom position of the pot and close the lid.
2. Spin the SmartSwitch™ to RAPID COOKER. Select the STEAM/ CRISP function, set the temperature to 175°C and set time for six mins on each side.
3. Next, click START/STOP to begin cooking. Divide the fish between plates and serve right away!

 Prep + Cooking Time: 13 mins

 Portions: 6

Ingredients:

- Four boneless salmon fillets
- 5g ground cumin
- 2g sweet paprika
- 2g chili powder
- 15ml olive oil
- 1.5g garlic powder
- Juice of one lime
- Salt & black pepper

Saffron Shrimp Mix

Preparation Steps:

1. Mix the shrimp with all the other items on the bottom of the unit; toss well and close the lid. Flip the SmartSwitch™ to AIR FRY/STOVETOP.
2. Select AIR FRY, set the temperature to 195°C and time also for eight mins. To start or stop cooking, press START/STOP.
3. Distribute among plates, then warmly serve.

Ingredients:

  Prep + Cooking Time: 18 mins

Portions: 3

- Twenty peeled and deveined shrimp
- 15g chopped parsley
- Four minced garlic cloves
- 30ml melted butter
- 0.35g saffron powder
- Juice of one lemon
- Salt & black pepper

Wonderful salmon fllets

Preparation Steps:

1. Place the trout on the bottom of the unit and add all other elements; rub the trout gently.
2. Lock up the lid and flip the SmartSwitch™ to RAPID COOKER. Select STEAM/CRISP, set temperature to 180°C and time to thirteen mins.
3. Divide between plates and serve

 Prep + Cooking Time: 23 mins

 Portions: 3

Ingredients:

- Two boneless trout fillets
- A chopped red chili pepper
- 1 tbsp. minced garlic
- 15ml lemon juice
- 15ml olive oil
- Salt & black pepper

Chilli Salmon Fillets

Preparation Steps:

1. Combine all the ingredients in a bowl, and toss and coat the fish well.
2. Transfer everything to your Speedi machine on the crisper tray in the bottom position and lock up the lid.
3. Flip the SmartSwitch™ to RAPID COOKER. Select STEAM & CRISP, set the temperature to 185°C for eight mins and click START/STOP to begin cooking; flipping the fish halfway.
4. Serve right away!

 Prep + Cooking Time: 16 mins

 Portions: 4

Ingredients:

- Two boneless salmon fillets
- Three chopped red chili peppers.
- 30ml lemon juice
- 15g minced garlic
- 30ml olive oil
- Salt & black pepper

Roasted Cod and Parsley

Preparation Steps:

1. Place the cod fillets on the crisper tray in the bottom position of the pot.
2. In a bowl, merge all other ingredients and whisk well.
3. Spread this mix over the fish and lock up the lid.
4. Next, flip the SmartSwitch™ to RAPID COOKER. STEAM/CRISP set the temperature to 200°C and time for ten mins, then press START/ STOP to begin cooking. Divide the fish between plates and serve

Ingredients:

- Four boneless medium cod filets
- A chopped shallot
- 1/4 cup melted butter
- Two minced garlic cloves
- 3 tbsp. chopped parsley
- 30ml lemon juice
- Salt & black pepper

 Prep + Cooking Time: 20 mins

Portions: 4

Side Dish
Recipes

Chapter: 6

Mixed Peppers Dish

Preparation Steps:

1. Mix all elements in the bottom of the pot; toss and close the lid. Flip the SmartSwitch™ to AIR FRY/STOVETOP. Select SEAR/SAUTE, set temperature to 180°C and time to twenty mins.
2. Press the START/STOP button to begin cooking.
3. Divide the peppers between plates and serve as a side dish.

 Prep + Cooking Time: 25 mins

 Portions: 3

Ingredients:

- Four red peppers; cut into medium strips
- Four green peppers; cut in medium strips
- A chopped red onion
- 5g smoked paprika
- 15ml olive oil
- Salt & black pepper

Fried Beans

Preparation Steps:

1. Mix all items except the coriander in the bottom of the unit; stir well and close the lid.
2. Flip the SmartSwitch™ to AIR FRY/STOVETOP. Select SEAR/SAUTE, set temperature to 195°C and time to a quarter-hour. Press START/STOP to begin cooking.
3. Finally, add the coriander, stir, divide between plates and serve as a side dish

  Prep + Cooking Time: 25 mins

Portions: 3

Ingredients:

- 160g drained canned chickpeas
- 945ml water
- 148g drained canned cranberry beans
- 185g blanched Runner beans
- A minced garlic clove
- Two chopped celery stalks
- A bunch of chopped coriander
- A chopped small red onion
- 75ml apple cider vinegar
- 60ml olive oil
- 15g sugar
- Salt & black pepper

Yellow Squash and Courgette

Preparation Steps:

1. In a bowl, combine all the items together, toss well and transfer everything to the crisper tray in the bottom position and close the lid.
2. The SmartSwitchTM should be programmed to AIR FRY/STOVETOP.
3. Pick DEHYDRATE, set the temperature to 205°C, and give it a 35-minute runtime. Divide between plates and serve as a side dish.

 Prep + Cooking Time: 35 mins

 Portions: 3

Ingredients:

- 455g sliced Courgette
- A yellow squash; halved, deseeded and cut in chunks
- 2g chopped coriander
- 15ml olive oil
- Salt & white pepper

Italian Mushroom

Preparation Steps:

1. In your Speedi meal machine, mix all the ingredients in the bottom position and toss well.
2. Close the lid, flip the SmartSwitch™ to AIR FRY/STOVETOP and select AIR FRY, set the temperature to 180°C then set the time also to a quarter-hour.
3. Divide the mix between plates and serve.

 Prep + Cooking Time: 25 mins

Portions: 3

Ingredients:

- 455g halved button mushrooms
- 45ml melted butter
- 5g grated parmesan cheese
- 5g Italian seasoning
- A pinch of salt & black pepper

Creamy Risotto

Preparation Steps:

1. Start by adding all ingredients except the coriander to the bottom of the unit and lock up the lid.
2. Flip the SmartSwitch™ to RAPID COOKER. Select STEAM, set temperature to 180°C and time to twenty mins.
3. Finally, add the coriander, stir, divide between plates and serve.

 Prep + Cooking Time: 30 mins

 Portions: 3

Ingredients:

- 225g sliced mushrooms
- 115g Double cream
- 400g risotto rice
- 945ml chicken stock; heated up
- Two minced garlic cloves
- A chopped yellow onion
- 15ml olive oil
- 2g chopped coriander
- 10g grated parmesan cheese

Smoked Aubergine

Preparation Steps:

1. Put all ingredients in the bottom of the unit; mix well and close the lid. Turn the SmartSwitchTM to the RAPID COOKER setting.
2. Locate STEAM, put the temperature to 195°C, and give it 20 minutes. Press START/STOP to begin cooking.
3. Divide between plates and serve as a side dish.

Prep + Cooking Time: 25 mins

Portions: 3

Ingredients:

- 680g cubed Aubergine
- 2g onion powder
- 2g sumac
- 15ml olive oil
- 3g za'atar
- Juice of one lime

Starter
Recipes

Chapter: 7

Cream Cheese Balls

Preparation Steps:

1. In a bowl, place all of the items and stir well.
2. Shape the mix into medium balls and then place them on the lined crisper tray in the bottom position and close the lid.
3. flip the SmartSwitch™ to AIR FRY/STOVETOP. Select AIR FRY, set the temperature to 190°C and put the time to five mins. Serve as a snack

 Prep + Cooking Time:15 mins

 Portions: 3

Ingredients:

- 115g cream cheese
- Fourteen chopped pepperoni slices
- Eight pitted and minced black olives
- 25g basil pesto
- 1g chopped basil
- Salt & black pepper

Refreshing lemony apple

Preparation Steps:

1. In the pot of your Speedi meal machine, mix all the ingredients; toss well and close the lid.
2. Flip the SmartSwitch™ to AIR FRY/STOVETOP. Select DEHYDRATE, set the temperature to 170°C and put the time to five mins.
3. Divide into cups and serve as a snack

Ingredients:

 Prep + Cooking Time: 10 mins

 Portions: 3

- Three big apples; cored, peeled and cubed
- 112ml caramel sauce
- 10ml lemon juice

Delicious Carrot Chips

Preparation Steps:

1. Put all of the items in a bowl and toss well, transfer the mixture to the crisper tray in the bottom position inside the pot and lock up the lid.
2. Flip the SmartSwitch™ to AIR FRY/STOVETOP.
3. Select DEHYDRATE, set the temperature to 190°C and put the time to twenty-five mins. Serve as a snack

  Prep + Cooking Time: 30 mins

Portions: 3

Ingredients:

- Four thinly sliced carrots
- 1g chaat masala
- 5ml olive oil
- 1g turmeric powder
- Salt & black pepper

Banana Chips

Preparation Steps:

1. On the crisper tray in the bottom position, put the banana slices and drizzle the oil over them then close the lid.
2. Flip the SmartSwitch™ to AIR FRY/STOVETOP. Select DEHYDRATE, set temperature to 180°C and time to five mins.
3. When the timer is finished, open the lid and transfer to bowls and serve them dipped in peanut butter.

 Prep + Cooking Time: 10 mins

 Portions: 3

Ingredients:

- A banana; peeled and sliced into sixteen pieces
- 60g soft peanut butter
- 15ml vegetable oil

Minced beef Bites

Preparation Steps:

1. In the beginning, mix panko with coconut in a bowl and stir well. In another bowl, mix the remaining elements and then shape medium meatballs out of this mixture.
2. Dredge the meatballs in the of mixture coconut and panko, put them on a crisper tray in the bottom position and close the lid.
3. Flip the SmartSwitch™ to AIR FRY/STOVETOP. Select SEARE/SAUTE, set temperature to 175°C and time also to a quarter-hour. Serve and enjoy!

Ingredients:

- 455g ground beef
- 3g garlic powder
- Two eggs
- 80g panko breadcrumbs
- 55g shredded coconut
- A drizzle of olive oil
- Salt & black pepper

 Prep + Cooking Time: 20 mins

 Portions: 4

Broccoli Bites

Preparation Steps:

1. On the lined bottom of the unit, spread the broccoli florets then add all other items; toss and lock up the lid.
2. Flip the SmartSwitch™ to AIR FRY/STOVETOP. Select AIR FRY, set the temperature to 230°C and set the time for a quarter-hour.
3. Divide into bowls and serve as a snack

Ingredients:

- A broccoli head; florets separated
- 5ml olive oil
- 5ml melted butter
- 3g garlic powder
- Salt & black pepper

 Prep + Cooking Time: 18 mins

 Portions: 3

Vegetable
Recipes

Chapter: 8

Hot Greek Potatoes

Preparation Steps:

1. Combine the pepper with the salt, potatoes, paprika and oil in a bowl; toss well and close the lid.
2. Flip the SmartSwitch™ to RAPID COOKER. Select STEAM, set temperature to 205°C and time to fifteen mins. Press START/STOP to begin cooking Transfer the potatoes to the serving dish and add the black olives and yoghurt.
3. Toss, serve and enjoy

Ingredients:

- 680g peeled and cubed potatoes
- 280g Greek yogurt
- 15ml olive oil
- 7g hot paprika
- 2g pitted and sliced black olives
- Salt & black pepper

 Prep + Cooking Time: 20 mins

 Portions: 3

Spinach and Cream Cheese

Preparation Steps:

1. On the bottom of your Speedi machine, mix all elements and toss gently then lock up the lid.
2. Next, Flip the SmartSwitch™ to AIR FRY/STOVETOP. Select SEAR/SAUTE, set temperature to 125 °C, and set time to eight mins. Press START/STOP to begin cooking.
3. When the cook is completed, divide between plates and serve!

Ingredients:

Prep + Cooking Time: 18 mins

Portions: 3

- 395g baby spinach
- 85g softened cream cheese
- One chopped yellow onion
- 15ml olive oil
- 30ml milk
- Salt & black pepper

Creamy asparagus gratin

Preparation Steps:

1. In the pot of your Speedi Meal machine, mix garlic with the asparagus, sour cream, garlic powder and cream cheese; toss.
2. Next, sprinkle the cheddar cheese on top and close the lid. Flip the SmartSwitch™ to AIR FRY/STOVETOP. Select SEAR/SAUTE, set temperature to 205°C and set time to six mins then press START.
3. Divide between plates; serve and enjoy!!

Ingredients:

 Prep + Cooking Time: 12 mins

 Portions: 3

- 395g trimmed asparagus
- 455g grated cheddar cheese
- 225g softened cream cheese
- Three minced garlic cloves
- 125g sour cream
- 2.5g garlic powder

Roasted fennel with garlic

Preparation Steps:

1. Combine all ingredients in a bowl; toss.
2. Transfer the fennel to the bottom of the unit and close the lid.
3. Next, flip the SmartSwitch™ to AIR FRY/STOVETOP. Select AIR FRY, set temperature to 205°C and set time to twelve mins, then press START to begin cooking.
4. Divide between plates and serve

Ingredients:

- Two trimmed and halved fennel bulbs
- 6g sweet paprika
- 15ml lime juice
- Two minced garlic cloves
- A drizzle of olive oil

 Prep + Cooking Time: 22 mins

 Portions: 4

Squash Salad

Preparation Steps:

1. Start by adding the squash to the crisper in the bottom position.
2. Add the oil, salt and pepper; toss well and lock up the lid.
3. Flip the SmartSwitch™ to AIR FRY/STOVETOP. Select AIR FRY, set temperature to 205°C and time to twelve mins, then press START to begin cooking. Transfer the squash to a bowl, add the coriander and vinegar and toss.
4. Serve and enjoy!

  Prep + Cooking Time: 18 mins

Portions: 4

Ingredients:

- A cubed butternut squash
- A chopped bunch coriander
- 30ml balsamic vinegar
- 15ml olive oil
- Salt & black pepper

Spicy Cabbage

Preparation Steps:

1. Mix all of the items on the bottom of your Speedi machine and lock up the lid.
2. Flip the SmartSwitch™ to AIR FRY/STOVETOP. Select SEAR/SAUTE, set temperature to 160°C, and set time to twelve mins.
3. Click START/STOP to begin cooking. Divide between plates and serve right away!!

Ingredients:

- A green shredded cabbage head
- 15ml olive oil
- 5g sweet paprika
- 1g cayenne pepper
- A pinch of salt & black

  Prep + Cooking Time: 18 mins

Portions: 3

Dessert
Recipes

Chapter: 9

Candied apple wedges

Preparation Steps:

1. On the bottom of the unit, mix the sugar with the butter and the apples; toss and close the lid.
2. Flip the SmartSwitch™ to AIR FRY/STOVETOP. Select AIR FRY, set temperature to 190°C and time to fifteen mins.
3. Serve warm

 Prep + Cooking Time: 20 mins

 Portions: 3

Ingredients:

- Four apples; peeled, cored and cut into wedges
- 45ml melted butter
- 40g cinnamon sugar

Pineapple and Carrot Cake

Preparation Steps:

1. In a bowl, place all of the elements (except the cooking spray) and combine well.
2. Grease your spring form pan that fits your Speedi machine with cooking spray, then pour the mixture inside. Lock up the lid and flip the SmartSwitch™ to RAPID COOKER.
3. Select STEAM & BAKE, set the temperature to 160°C, and give it 45 minutes.
4. To start, press START/STOP. Serve it cold.

 Prep + Cooking Time: 55 mins

 Portions: 4

Ingredients:

- 140g flour
- 50g pineapple juice
- 30g grated carrots
- 25g shredded coconut flakes
- 50g sugar
- One whisked egg
- 45g yoghurt
- 60ml vegetable oil
- 5g baking powder
- 5g Bicarbonate of soda
- 2g cinnamon powder
- Cooking spray

Delicious lemon Cake

Preparation Steps:

1. In a bowl, mix well all elements together.
2. Pour this mix into a greased cake pan and put it in your Speedi machine and close the lid.
3. Flip the SmartSwitch™ to RAPID COOKER. Choose STEAM & BAKE, set the temperature to 160°C, put the time to seventeen mins then press START to begin cooking.
4. Let the cake cool and enjoy!!

 Prep + Cooking Time: 22 mins

 Portions: 4

Ingredients:

- 85g Light brown sugar
- 85g flour
- 130ml melted butter
- Three eggs
- 3g grated dark chocolate
- 2.5ml lemon juice

Orange Cake

Preparation Steps:

1. Place all of the items in a bowl and merge well.
2. Divide the mixture between three ramekins and place them in your Speedi machine and close the lid.
3. Flip the SmartSwitch™ to RAPID COOKER. Choose STEAM & BAKE, set the temperature to 160°C, and the time also at twenty mins.
4. Serve the cakes warm and enjoy!

Ingredients:

- 60g flour
- Two egg
- 15ml orange juice
- 60g sugar
- 30ml vegetable oil
- 60ml milk
- 10g cocoa powder
- 1g orange zest
- 3g baking powder

 Prep + Cooking Time: 30 mins

 Portions: 4

Yummy Rice Pudding

Preparation Steps:

1. Put all ingredients on the bottom of the unit; stir well and lock up the lid.
2. Flip the SmartSwitch™ to AIR FRY/STOVETOP. Choose AIR FRY, set the temperature to 180°C and determine time to twenty mins then press START/STOP to begin cooking.
3. Stir the pudding, divide it into bowls, refrigerate and serve cold.

Ingredients:

- 200g white rice
- 455ml milk
- 35g sugar
- 15ml melted butter
- 15g Double cream
- 5g vanilla extract

Prep + Cooking Time: 20 mins

Portions: 3

Printed in Great Britain
by Amazon

33524565R00044